AF426627

JESUS NEVER
TAUGHT THE TRINITY

Written in the light of the Bible,
the Quran and other reliable sources

Dil R. Banu

DIL R. BANU / Tasneem Media LLC
9905 Ashburton Ln
Bethesda, MD 20817
(301-706-0739 / 301-732-9648)
dilbanu90@gmail.com
www.godinbibleandquran.com

This book is a work of theological and scriptural commentary. It contains extensive comparative analysis of religious doctrines, particularly the Christian doctrine of the Trinity, as interpreted through the texts of the Holy Bible and the Holy Quran. It reflects the author's research in comparative religion and should be considered a scholarly inquiry into historical and religious texts.

ISBN(s):
Paperback: 979-8-89175-196-5
eBook: 979-8-89175-197-2

Ordering Information:
Quantity sales. Special discounts are available on quantity purchases by corporations, associations, and others. For details, contact the "Special Sales Department" at the address above.

DEDICATION

To the believers in God and the seekers for truth.

TABLE OF CONTENTS

ACKNOWLEDGEMENTS

I'd first thank God-my Creator-Lord most humbly, gratefully, and endlessly to choose me for this noble job of writing and to help me complete it under His constant care and guidance. I also beg Him to kindly forgive me for all my negligence and mistakes that I might have shown or done due to my own ignorance and shortcomings.

I also ask God fervently to shower His endless mercy, love, and blessing for all the authors and religious scholars alive and dead, who helped me to write this book with valuable information and material which they obtained through their ceaseless effort, study, and research. I have added a list of their books in a bibliography at the end of my book.

I also like to offer my heartfelt thanks to all my learned reviewers who, despite their busy schedule, made some time to read the manuscript of my book and to write a few encouraging words to enhance its worth.

I would like to appreciate my wonderful daughter Tasmeea and son Shihab along with their most adorable spouses and children for their constant help, care, and support to continue with my study and writing undisturbed. May God kindly ensure for them a safe, secure, and a happy life both here and hereafter.

Last but not the least, my special thanks and gratitude goes to my college-going beloved grandson Abid Noor for his constant help and support to publish this book.

Salutation to Prophet Muhammad and other prophets of God who were sent before him

I'd like to remind all my Muslim friends to ask God to shower His endless mercy and blessing upon Prophet Muhammad and other Prophets before him when they come across with their blessed names.

WHAT MADE ME WRITE THIS BOOK

I am a Muslim by birth and practice. I wrote this book mainly for the devoted Christians who made Jesus an object of worship along with God or as one of the Gods in the Trinity. While reading the Quran which God has sent through His last Prophet Muhammad for the guidance of all mankind, I first came to know about this unique doctrine where the Christians worship One God in the union of three. From the meaning and the interpretation of the verses 4:171 and 5:72-73 in the Quran, I understood the Christians worship God as the Father, Jesus as His only begotten and the Holy Ghost or the Holy Spirit as One or the Same God.

The Quran has also reminded us repeatedly that Jesus never taught his people to worship him as God or as one of the Gods in the Trinity. Rather, he taught them to believe in One God and to worship none but Him as did all his Predecessors before him. Interestingly, I found those statements in the Quran true to the letter when I read the Bible, especially the Gospel of Jesus for the first time in my life. I mean while reading the Gospel, I didn't come across a single verse where Jesus asked his people to worship him as God or along with God in any form or manner. Not only that, the entire Bible also does not have a single statement with the word trinity. It was then I became truly curious to know how the doctrine of the Trinity became an indispensable part of Christian Faith, if Jesus had never taught it and even the entire Bible had no mention of it?

To appease my curiosity, I decided to ask about it to my Christian missionary friends who used to visit me often at my residence. The main purpose of their visit was to tell me how I could get rid of my sin and have eternal life in heaven only through having faith in Jesus as my savior. Then for the sake of truth, I needed to tell them about the basic requirements of our faith. I told them that as Muslims or followers of Prophet Muhammad, we must worship none but One God as our Creator-Lord, our true Guide, Savior and the Disposer of all our affairs both here and hereafter. Besides that, it is also an indispensable part of our faith to believe in all the prophets of God beginning from Adam to His last Prophet Muhammad and in all His scriptures that He revealed upon them. Accordingly, we believe Jesus was a mighty Messenger of God and he was sent last with the Gospel from the House of Israel for the guidance of his own people-the misguided Jews. I also told them that we also believe man is accountable for his own sin and nobody can forgive his sin except God whom we call Allah.

Sometimes, while talking to my missionary friends about the differences of our faith in Jesus, I used to ask them straight how they worship three Gods being One or the same. It was then I noticed that none of them felt comfortable talking about it. Not only that, they also wanted to leave soon with some plausible excuses. Finally, one of them who became a close friend of mine through her frequent visits, agreed to answer my question. This book is written mainly on the long conversation that I had with her about the doctrine of the Trinity.

I think the open-minded and the truth-seeking Christians will feel interested to know how the Trinity became an obligatory part of their faith if Jesus never preached or practiced it himself, nor the entire Bible had any evidence for it. I hope this book will help them to find the answer with information and evidence from the Bible, the Quran and other reliable sources.

DIL R BANU
Maryland,
September 2025

SUMMARY OF THE CONTENTS

Chapter One: Both parts of the Bible proclaim: God is one and to worship none but Him

- Men knew God as their Only Lord and about His path right from the beginning
- God made His everlasting covenant with Abraham and with all his generations after him
- All the prophets in the Old Testament taught their people to worship none but One God and to obey His Commands
- Jesus also asked his people to worship none but One God and to strive for their eternal life through keeping His commands
- Jesus has made the status of God highest of all through his own words and deeds
- Jesus' own words and deeds are sufficient to prove he was but a man of flesh and blood
- The Quran-the last and the final Scripture of God also said the same about Jesus and his teaching

Chapter Two: Jesus never taught the Trinity, it was invented after he left

- Three of them, the Father, the Son and the Holy Spirit are made of the same substance
- Trinity to be understood in three states of water
- Jesus had power over entire heavens and earth

- Jesus admitted himself no one was aware of the last hour except God
- The statement in 1 John 5:7 has been discarded as unauthentic
- The Trinity was a manmade product approved by the Council of Nicaea
- Whoever wishes to be saved must, above all, keep the Catholic faith
- Christian Truth is different from Christian Religion
- The Unitarian Christians rejected the Trinity as a lie and faced inhuman sufferings because of that
- The Quran has denounced the Trinity as a clear blaspheme against the oneness of God
- My own reflection after I learned the Christians still worship the Trinity as a way to their salvation

CHAPTER ONE

Both parts of the Bible proclaim: God is one and to worship none but Him

Hear, O Israel: The Lord our God is one Lord. And thou shalt love the Lord thy God, with all thine heart, and with all thy soul, and with all thy might. (Duet 6:4-5)

Before I enter into the main topic of our discussion, I like to tell my Christian friends that while writing my book ONE GOD FOR ALL, I needed to read both parts of the Bible minutely. It was then I learned that all the Prophets of God before Jesus taught their people to believe in One God, to worship none but Him and to strive for their eternal life through keeping His commands that He sent through them for their guidance. Jesus also did the same when God sent him as His last Prophet from the House of Israel for the guidance of his own people meaning the Jews who deviated then largely from the laws of the Torah.

I think my Christian friends will understand my point much better if I provide some evidence first from the Old Testament of the Bible, and then from the Gospel-the Book they claim as a true account of Jesus' own words and deeds. I have quoted those verses mostly from the Bible of King James Version and some of them from the Bible of New International Version.

Men knew God as their Only Lord and about His path right from the beginning

We may start with Genesis, the first book of Moses in the Old Testament:

> : *In the beginning, God created the heavens and the earth…. And the LORD God formed man of the dust of the ground and breathed into his nostrils the breath of life; and man became a living soul.* (Gen 1:1; 2:7)

> : *But Noah found grace in the eyes of the LORD. These are the generations of Noah: Noah was a just man and perfect in his generations, and Noah walked with God.* (Gen 6:8–9)

The first two verses confirm that no one existed in the beginning except God Who created heaven and earth and then He formed Adam-the father of mankind out of dust and made him a complete human being after He breathed His spirit through his nostrils. The next verse tells us the path of God was defined from the start and the spread of human habitation, but it was followed only by just and righteous persons like Noah.

God made His everlasting covenant with Abraham and with all his generations after him

From the following verses of the Genesis, we came to know that God made His Everlasting covenant with Abraham and with all his generations after him.

> : *And when Abram* [Abraham] *was ninety years old and nine, the LORD appeared to Abram, and said unto him, I am the Almighty God; walk before me, and be thou perfect.* (Gen17:1)

> *: And I will establish my covenant between me and thee and thy seed after thee in their generations for an everlasting covenant, to be a God unto thee, and to thy seed after thee.* (Gen17:7)

By this everlasting covenant, God meant Abraham and all his descendants will worship Him as their only LORD. It is in fact, pure monotheism or the fundamental truth in the guidance of God that He revealed to all His Messengers beginning from Adam to His last Prophet Muhammad. But as I know the devoted followers of Jesus Christ only believe in the Bible as the words of God, I shall try to provide evidence from both Parts of the Bible to justify the truth of my claim.

All the prophets in the Old Testament taught their people to worship none but One God and to obey His Commands

In the following verses of the Old Testament, we shall find that all the prophets of God from Moses to Malachi taught their people to worship only One God and to obey His commands that He revealed through them. Out of countless verses, I've quoted below only a few of them.

God said to Moses-one of His mighty Prophets from the House of Israel:

> *: I am the LORD. And I appeared unto Abraham, unto Isaac, and unto Jacob, by the name of God Almighty, but by my name Jehovah was I not known to them.* (Exodus 6:2–3)

> *: Ye shall do my judgments, and keep mine ordinances, to walk therein: I am the LORD your God.* (Lev 18:4)

Moses also said to his people:

: Know therefore this day, and consider it in thine heart, that the LORD he is God in heaven above, and upon the earth beneath there is none else. (Duet 4:39)

: Hear, O Israel, The LORD our God is one LORD. And thou shalt love the LORD thy God with all thine heart, and with all thy soul, and with all thy might. (Duet 6:4-5)

: Ye shall diligently keep the commandments of the LORD your God, and His testimonies, and His statutes, which He hath commanded thee. (Duet 6:17)

: If you ever forget the LORD your God and follow other gods and worship and bow down to them, I testify against you today that you will surely be destroyed. (Duet 8:19)

In the following verses of the Old Testament, David-a mighty king and a Prophet of God from the House of Israel has also expressed his unconditional love, devotion, and gratitude to God in appreciation of His endless glory, greatness, compassion, kindness and above all, for His being the only True Guide, Savior, and Refuge to him.

: How great you are, Sovereign LORD! There is no one like you, and there is no God but you, as we have heard with our own ears. (2 Samuel 7:22)

: The LORD is my rock, my fortress, and my deliverer; my God is my rock, in whom I take refuge, my shield and the horn of my salvation. He is my stronghold, my refuge, and my savior … (2 Samuel 22: 2-3)

God has also described through His other Messengers about His oneness, absolute power, authority and knowledge over everything in the entire heavens and earth, as well as about His endless love, mercy, and compassion for all of mankind.

: I, even I, am the LORD; and beside me there is no savior. (Isa 43:11)

> : …..*And there is no God else besides me, a just God and a Savior; there is none beside me.* (Isa 45:21)

> : *Can anyone hide himself in secret places that I shall not see him? Saith the LORD. Do not I fill heaven and earth? Saith the LORD.* (Jeremiah 23:24)

> : *And, go not for other gods to serve them, and to worship them, and provoke me not to anger with the works of your hands; and I will do you no hurt.* (Jeremiah 25:6)

> : *Yet I am the LORD thy God from the land of Egypt, and thou shalt know no god but me: for there is no savior beside me.* (Hos13:4)

> : *Even now, declares the LORD, return to me with all your heart, with fasting and weeping, and mourning: Rend your heart and not your garments. Return to the LORD your God, for he is gracious and compassionate, slow to anger, and abounding in love…* (Joel 2:12–13)

God says through Malachi-His last Prophet mentioned in the Old Testament of the Bible:

> : *Remember the law of my servant Moses, the decrees, and laws I gave him at Horeb for all Israel.* (Mal 4:4)

I think the message in the above-quoted verses is simple and clear and no explanation is required to convince my readers especially my Christian friends that all the Prophets of God who were sent before Jesus were commanded to teach their people to worship none but One God as their Creator-Lord, True Guide, their only Savior and the Disposer of all their affairs. In addition to that, they also taught their people to strive for their eternal life through keeping the commands of God. While reading the Gospel, I also came across many verses where Jesus is seen to teach the same to his people as did all his predecessors before him. The truth can be checked in the following statements of the Gospel.

Jesus also asks his people to worship none but One God and to strive for their eternal life through keeping His commands

> : *And Jesus answered him* [a Jewish scribe who asked him what is the first commandment of all], *the first of all the commandments is, Hear, O Israel, the LORD our GOD is ONE LORD: And thou shalt love the LORD thy GOD with all thy heart, and with all thy soul, and with all thy mind, and with all thy strength: this is the first commandment.* (Mark 12:29-30)

> : *Jesus gave them this answer: "Very truly I tell you, the Son can do nothing by himself; he can do only what he sees his Father doing, because whatever the Father does, the Son also does.* (John 5:19)

> : *My Father which gave them me, is greater than all.*(John 10:29)…*If ye loved me, ye would rejoice, because I said, I go unto the Father: For my Father is greater than I.* (John 14:28)

> : *Very truly I tell you, no servant is greater than his master, nor is a messenger greater than the one who sent him.* (John 13:16)

> : *But about that day or hour no one knows, not even the angels in heaven, nor the Son, but only the Father.* (Mark 13:32)

> : *Then said Jesus, Father, Father, forgive them; for they know not what they do.* (Luke 23:34)

If Jesus knew he were God, or His equal, he certainly couldn't make those statements where he has admitted to the people openly that God is greater than all and him, too. Neither would he call him a servant and God as his Master. Nor could he say that he was not able to do anything but by the will and the command of God. Besides that, if Jesus were God or an inseparable part of God as his devoted followers claim about him, he could never tell them he was not aware of the Last Hour meaning the end of the existing world. As he was a true Messenger of God, he admitted himself honestly that no one was aware of the Last Hour except God.

Similarly, Jesus would never ask God to forgive the sin of the wrongdoers if he knew all their sins will be forgiven completely through sacrifice of his life on the Cross as it is believed by his devoted followers as an indispensable part of their faith.

Besides that, the following verses of the Gospel also tells us that Jesus used to pray to God himself and to teach his disciples how to pray to God and what to ask Him in their prayer.

> *: And it came to pass in those days, that he* (Jesus) *went out into a mountain to pray and continued all night in prayer to God.* (Luke 6:12)

> *: And being in an agony he prayed more earnestly: and his sweat was as it were great drops of blood falling down to the ground.* (Luke 22:44)

> *: And he said unto them* [his disciples], *"When you pray, say: 'Father, hallowed be your name, Your kingdom come. Give us each day our daily bread. Forgive us our sins, for we also forgive everyone who sins against us. And lead us not into temptation.* (Luke 11:2–4)

In the quoted verses above, it is clear to all that Jesus often prayed to God, and he prayed to Him more when he was in distress. Not only that he also taught his disciples how to pray to God and what to pray to Him. At this point, a sensible reader might ask in wonder, does the Almighty and All-knowing God may ever go through any kind of distress or agony as a man does? Or does God ever pray to Himself to remove His distress? Besides that, if Jesus and God were one and the same, and both were in distress, in that case who prayed to whom to get rid of that? I think these sorts of unpleasant but unavoidable questions arise when we believe and worship God by the invented doctrines of men and give up what He commanded us to do through all His designated Messengers.

Jesus' own words and deeds are sufficient to prove he was a man of flesh and blood

In the following statements of the Gospel, Jesus' own words and deeds are sufficient to prove that he was a man of flesh and blood and he was also a dedicated Prophet of God.

> *: Going a little farther, he* [Jesus] *fell with his face to the ground and prayed, "My father, if it is possible, may this cup be taken from me. Yet not as I will, but as you will.* (Math 26:39)

> *: He went away a second time and prayed, "My father, if it is not possible for this cup to be taken away unless I drink it, may your will be done." (Math 26:42)*

In the quoted statements, Jesus made it clear to all that he was but a man of flesh and blood, and at the same time he was also a dedicated Messenger of God. First, as a human being, Jesus expressed his anguish when he understood his arrest and persecution by the Roman authority was imminent. Then as a dedicated Servant or a Messenger of God, he submitted himself completely to His will and command and became ready to accept gracefully what his Lord had destined for him. Despite that, Jesus felt himself deserted of the mercy of God at his last moment on the Cross and cried to Him grieving:

> *: About three in the afternoon Jesus cried out in a loud voice, "Eli, Eli, lama sabachthani?"* [in Aramaic which means "My God, my God, why have you forsaken me"?] (Matthew 27:46)

I think this one statement of Jesus is enough to prove he was not God or his equal, but a mortal human being who fears death and depends entirely on the mercy of his Lord to overcome it. I hope no more evidence is required to prove that Jesus was a human being whom God made unique and special through his birth without a father and chose him as His Prophet from the House of Israel for the guidance of his own people.

The Quran-the final Scripture of God also said the same about Jesus and about his teaching

Interestingly, the Quran-the last and the final Scripture of God, which was sent to Prophet Muhammad more than fourteen hundred years ago also describes the same about Jesus. I mean the Quran also tells us that Jesus was unique and special because of his miraculous birth and God chose him as His Prophet from the House of Israel for the guidance of his own people. Out of countless verses, I've quoted below only a few of them for both my Christian and non-Christian friends where they will find who Jesus really was, what exactly he taught his people, what he never taught and what his people did in his name after he left.

> *"O Mary! Verily, Allah* [Allah is the name of God in Arabic] *gives you the glad tidings of a Word from Him: his name will be Christ Jesus, son of Mary.* (3:45)

> *: She* [Mary] *said: 'O my Lord! How shall I have a son when no man has ever touched me?' He said: 'Even so. God creates what He wills; when He decides to do anything, He only says to it, 'Be' and it is!* (3:47)

> *: And He will teach him the Book, wisdom, and the Torah and Injeel. And He will make him a Messenger to the children of Israel.......* (3:48-49)

> *: Christ-the son of Mary was no more than a Messenger of God. There were many apostles who passed away before him. His mother was a truthful woman.* (5:75)

: And when Jesus came with clear proofs, he said: "I have come to you with prophethood, and to make clear to you some of the points on which you differ. Therefore, fear Allah and obey me. Verily, Allah! He is my Lord and your Lord. So, worship Him Alone. This is the Straight Path. (43: 63-64)

: [Jesus said to his people] *I am appointed to confirm that which is before me from the Torah and to make lawful to you some of the things forbidden to you. Now I have brought the signs from your Lord, therefore fear God, and obey me. In fact, Allah is my Lord as well as your Lord, therefore, Worship Him; this is the right Way.* (3:50-51)

: They [Christians] *say: 'Allah has begotten a son!' Glory be to Him! He is self-sufficient! His is all that is in the heavens and earth! Have you any proof for what you say? Would you ascribe to Allah something about which you have no knowledge?* (10:68)

: It is not befitting to the majesty of Allah that He should beget a son. Glory be to Him! When He determines a matter, He only says to it 'Be' and it is. (19:35)

: They disbelieve who say: "God is one of the 'three' in a Trinity." For, there is no god except One God. If they desist not from what they say, verily a grievous chastisement will befall the disbelievers among them. (5:73)

I think the verses I quoted above from different parts of the Quran carry the same truth about Jesus that we already have learned from the Gospel. I mean the Quran-the last and the final scripture of God also confirms and testifies through His last Prophet Muhammad that Jesus was only a unique and special Messenger of God from the House of Israel and he also asked his people to worship none but One God and to obey His commands that he taught them from the Books of Torah and the Gospel. The Quran also tells us that Jesus never asked his people to worship him as God or along with God or as one of the Gods in the Trinity.

After I learned it from both Bible and Quran, I became very curious to know how the Trinity became a part of Christian faith if it was not taught by Jesus, or by any of his close companions, or by any other Prophet of God sent before him?

I invite my readers cordially to the next chapter to find the answer.

John said, "Do not hold on to me, for I have not yet ascended to the Father. Go instead to my brothers and tell them, I am ascending to my Father and your Father, to my God and your God. (John 20:17)

CHAPTER TWO

Jesus Never Taught the Trinity, It was Invented After He Left

For there are three that bear record in heaven, the Father, the Word, and the Holy Ghost: And these three are one. (1 John 5:7)

To appease my curiosity, I saved my question about the Trinity for my Christian missionary friends who used to visit me often at my residence mainly in the late morning of Saturday. But my question remained unanswered for a long time because I noticed most of them seemed to be uncomfortable to talk about it, and to leave me soon with some excuses when I asked them to explain the Trinity or how they worship three Gods as One or the Same?

Finally, Mrs. Robinson-a middle-aged white lady, one of my old missionary friends agreed to answer my question when she visited me once at my residence on a Saturday morning. She already knew about my interest in the study of the Bible and especially about my love and respect for Jesus from the perspective of my faith as a Muslim. She also knew I was writing a book on Jesus based on the narration of the Bible and the Quran both. So, I felt she would be the right person to talk about it. But from my previous experience with my other missionary friends, I felt I needed to be cautious and careful to raise the issue of the Trinity to her as a topic of my discussion.

So, after I welcomed her in cordially, and sat comfortably in our living room, I began to enquire about her health, family, job, her trip to Arizona to visit her newly married sister, and then I said to her cheerfully, "Mrs. Robinson, I think you are Godsent."

"Really? May I know why?"

"Sure. I've been reading the Gospel for the last few days only to know about the Trinity, but I didn't find it anywhere. I think you could help me to find it. Right?"

To my surprise, she agreed and said, "I may try." Then she took out her Bible in the King James Version from her handbag and started turning the pages and stopped towards the end of the Book. Then she said "You will find it in 1 John, verse 7 in chapter 5."

Luckily, I also had the same version of the Bible, and it was on the center-table along with a copy of the Quran and other books on religion. Before I opened my Bible, I said to her politely, "Mrs. Robinson, I think you know that I'm writing a book on Jesus from the narration of both Bible and Quran. Will you mind if I write about this topic based on our discussion?"

Mrs. Robinson looked at me for a moment, seemed to be a bit hesitant, and then said smiling, "No, not at all; but you have to give me a copy when it is published."

"Sure, you will be the first person to get it. Now please tell me again the name of the Book, the number of the chapter, and the verse." I said while turning the pages of the Bible on my lap.

"The Book is 1John, chapter 5, and the verse is 7."

"Yes, I got it. You may now read." I said to her after I found it. Mrs. Robinson began to read in her soft, sweet and well- modulated voice,

*: For there are three that bear record in heaven, the Father,
the Word, and the Holy Ghost: And these three are one.*

After she finished reading, I said: "Please excuse me for my shortcomings, because I don't see where in this verse, you are told to worship the Father, the Word, and the Holy Ghost as One God?"

"It is understood."

"Will you please explain a bit?"

From her slow and laconic explanation, I came to know that Father is God as the Godhead; the Word is God as His only begotten Son Jesus; and there is also the Holy Ghost or the Holy Spirit along with them. These three are merged into one. Thus, the Christians worship one God in the union of three.

But I remained in the dark as before.

So, I said to her again apologetically, "Please don't mind, it still sounds to me very confusing, because I think to be worshiped like God, Jesus and the Holy Ghost should also be like God. I mean, both Jesus and the Holy Ghost must have the same essence and attributes of God to deserve our worship. Don't you think so, too?"

Three of them are made of the same substances

"Sure. We believe," Mrs. Robinson continued, "The Father, the Son, and the Holy Spirit are made of the same substance, and because of that they have the same equal majesty and the glory of a fully independent God."

'But how do you know they are made of the same substance? Can you provide any evidence from the Bible in support of that?' I was about to ask her, but I did not. I asked her instead, "But how do you worship three independent Gods as one independent God?"

"There lies the mystery. Despite their own independence, we worship them together as one Independent God."

"But how is it possible? I mean, how could they maintain their independence after they become united as one God?" I asked her again, trying to be very polite and patient.

"It is possible, because they are merged into one without losing their own independence."

The way she described, it seemed to me the God of the Trinity matched more with a very mysterious, magical, or a supernatural Being found in some modern digital movie, but it could no way match with One Almighty God of the Judeo-Christian Faith or with the God of Islam that we find in the narration of both Bible and Quran.

Besides that, a series of unwanted but unavoidable questions flashed in my mind one after another at the same time.

I wanted to ask her how 3 which is always 1 digit less than 4, and 1 digit more than 2, can be considered as 1?

I wanted to ask her how the Father, the Son, and the Holy Spirit function as a fully independent God after they are merged into one?

I wanted to ask her what is the use of being independent or having the same substance, glory, and majesty, if they cannot do anything separately? And, if they do, then what will happen to their unity?

I also wanted to ask her how they maintained their unity, when Jesus-one of the inseparable parts of the Trinity died on the Cross and remained buried for three days? Did the Godhead and the Holy Spirit die with him, too?

Then to distract myself from the flow of those unpalatable but unavoidable questions, I said to her again very politely, "Sorry, I still have no clue how these three independent Gods get merged into One God without losing their own independence or majesty."

Trinity to be understood in three states of water

"I know it is very difficult to understand," Mrs. Robinson sounded a little hesitant when she said, "Especially for the people of other faiths. Okay, let me try to explain it with an example. Just think of water in its three different states: liquid, solid, and steam. Water is liquid, ice is solid, and air is steam. Now, what is the substance we find common in the three of them?"

"Water, obviously."

"Similarly, the substance of three Gods is one and the same, just like the water is found common in its three different states. I hope now you know what it means."

"Sorry, I'm still confused, because we believe God is eternal and so is His essence and attributes. In that case, whatever His substance is, it should also remain with Him unchanged for eternity. Don't you think so, too?"

"Sure. It is what I meant when I gave you the example of water.

It also remains unchanged forever in its three different states."

"It is true, but I don't think this example is good enough to clarify the status of Three Independent Gods being worshiped as one God. Let me explain why. You said ice, water, and steam can be considered separate and the same because all three are composed of the same substance. But you also know very well that water does not remain the same in its three different states. For example, when water changes into ice, it loses its liquidity and when it turns into steam, it loses its liquidity and solidity both. Most important of all, water does not freeze into ice or change into steam on its own. It must go through certain states or conditions to become ice or steam, right?"

Mrs. Robinson did not answer.

Looking at her serene face, I continued, "But we believe the essence, attributes, or the substance of God remain the same or unchanged under all circumstances. Nothing could affect, change, or destroy them anyway. I mean, if God adds anything new to His creation, or eliminates anything from His creation, or changes anything to something else, His power of creativity always remains the same or intact. But how could we believe the same about Jesus whom you claim to die on the Cross? I mean, how could we consider him equal to God Who is Eternal and Ever-living?"

"Jesus is also eternal like his Father in Heaven, because the Gospel also tells us that he overcame death through his resurrection. Who but God has control over life and death?"

"Sure. I have no question about that. But you also believe Jesus' resurrection took place after three days of his burial. In that case how could you claim Jesus to be eternal like God Who never dies, sleeps, or remains unconscious even for a moment?"

"We believe so because after the resurrection, Jesus met with his disciples and promised to stay with them until the end of the world. Do you think Jesus would promise so, if he were not eternal like God?"

I certainly did not expect to hear it from her in support of Jesus' being eternal or equal to God. But as I needed to reach a conclusion of what I started myself, I must hold my patience until we come to that point. So I said to her, being cautious and careful, "I know you are talking about the last verse of the last Chapter in the Gospel of Matthew, right?"

> Teaching them to observe all things whatsoever I have commanded you. And, lo, I am with you, always, even unto the end of the world. A'-men. (Matthew 28:20)

"I appreciate your memory."

"Thanks. But my memory is not so good as you think. I already mentioned to you that I've been trying to find out where in the Gospel Jesus has taught his people to worship him as God or as one of the Gods in the Trinity. Now let me answer your question. You think Jesus is eternal like God because he promised to stay with his disciples until the end of the world, right?"

"Yes. It is what he said to them."

"Please excuse me if I think you took the apparent meaning of what Jesus said and overlooked its inherent message."

"May I please know what makes you think so?"

"I think so because I believe Jesus did not mean to stay with his disciples as the eternal God does. He meant to stay with them forever through his high morals, piety, and the commands of God that he left for them in the Gospel." I stopped here for a while, took a few sips of water from my water-bottle, and then said, "In fact, it is not only Jesus, but other Prophets of God like Abraham, Moses, Muhammad, and all the legendary figures in the history of the world, are still alive in the hearts of men through some of their great deeds or achievements. So, what do you think of them? Are they eternal too, as God is?"

Jesus had power over entire heavens and earth

"But they are not like Jesus," Mrs. Robinson tried to oppose nicely, "None of them had power like God, but Jesus had."

"How do you know Jesus had power like God?" I asked her in wonder.

"Jesus said it himself in the same chapter of Matthew you just mentioned. He said he had power over entire heavens and earth. Okay, let me read to you. You will find it in verse 18." Mrs. Robinson picked up her Bible from the side-table beside her and opened it.

"Sure." I also picked up my Bible and opened the last chapter in the Gospel of Matthew though I knew very well what she was going to read.

"Yes, here it is. May I read now?" Mrs. Robinson stopped turning the pages of the Bible and asked.

"Sure."

"Thanks." Then she began to read in her soft and sweet voice:

And Jesus came and spoke unto them, saying, 'All power is given unto me in heaven and in earth'. After she finished reading, she closed her Book and asked me politely, "Do you think Jesus could ever claim so, if he were not as powerful as God is?"

To speak the truth, I have read that verse before several times and I have my own explanation about it. So, I said to her casually but confidently, "I think you have overlooked one tiny but vital point that Jesus left in his claim."

"May I please know what that point is?"

"Sure. Jesus told his disciples that all power over the heavens and earth were given to him. It means Jesus had that power only after he received it from God, not before that. In that case, how could we claim the status of the Giver and the given is one or the same?"

"Sorry. I think we are too small to understand the mystery of this relation between the Father and the Son."

'Can you please tell me where you find the mystery when I see it is as clear as daylight?' I was about to ask her, but I did not, because from my long experience with my other missionary friends, I became familiar with the pattern of their thoughts and questions. I found whenever they lack reason in their argument, they try to cover it with the excuse of mystery. And when they talk about mystery, they try to avoid questions and become eager to leave with some plausible excuses. But I wanted her to stay, not to leave.

So, I said to her promptly, "Okay, it is for the sake of argument, let me believe Jesus was as powerful as God is. But it still does not make him God, because it does not tell us whether he was also All-Knowing as God is."

"It doesn't tell us either, he was not, right?" Mrs. Robinson asked me back very politely.

"I wish I could support you of what you just said. But I can't, because there are some statements in the Gospel where Jesus has made it clear to all that he was not All-knowing as God is. Let me provide some evidence to justify my point.

Jesus admitted himself no one was aware of the last day or hour except God

"Once talking to his disciples, Jesus admitted to them honestly that he was not aware of the Last day or Hour meaning when the world will end. He also told them that no one had any knowledge of that except God. Don't you think, if Jesus and God were One and the Same as you claim, he also knew about it?"

> But of that day and hour knoweth no man, no, not the angels in heaven, but my Father only. (Math 24:36)

Mrs. Robinson did not answer.

In her silence, I said to her, "I hope you also remember what happened when Jesus became hungry on the way to Jerusalem with his disciples. He saw a fig tree and went to it to appease his hunger, but he found the tree had the leaves but no fig. Then his disciples told him that it was not the season of fig. Doesn't it tell us that Jesus didn't even know the season......

"Would you please tell me then," Mrs. Robinson cut me off nicely, and asked, "Why Jesus commanded his disciples to baptize all nations in the name of the Father, the Son, and the Holy Ghost, if they were not one and the same?"

: Go ye therefore, and teach all nations, baptizing in the name of the Father, and of the Son, and of the Holy Ghost (Math 24:19)

I already mentioned before that I had been reading the Gospel minutely only to know about the Trinity and what really happened before and after Jesus was arrested and put on the Cross. It was then I came across that command of Jesus to his disciples whom he met in a mountain of Galilee after he rose up from his grave. Frankly speaking, I found that command of Jesus very strange and interesting. So, I devoted myself completely to know what he really meant by it. After some time, I felt I understood why Jesus said that to his disciples or what he really meant by it.

So, I thanked my guest in silence for her question and asked her back, "Madam, do you really believe that by this command, Jesus meant his disciples to teach the people to worship the Father, the Son, and the Holy Ghost as one God?"

"Isn't it most obvious? Otherwise, why have we been worshiping them as one God for the last two thousand years?"

'Do you think a wrong thing turns out to be right if it is believed to be right for thousands of years?' I was about to ask her but checked myself. From her question, I understood she was also one of them who claimed the Gospel as the true account of Jesus' own words and deeds, but never tried to understand what the Gospel had really said about him or about his teaching. At that moment, I also understood once again that our faith in God whether it is blind, or prudent, is equally strong and unshakable.

So, keeping my question to myself, I said to her slowly, softly, and choosing my words carefully, "Yes, I agree. Our intelligence is too short to comprehend the mystery in the words or the acts of God. So, let's go back to the main topic of our discussion. If you really believe Jesus wanted his disciples to teach the people to worship the Father, the Son, and the Holy Spirit as One God, in that case, it is very much expected that he taught them about it long before he was arrested by the Roman soldiers. Right?"

"May I please know what difference it makes?" Mrs. Robinson asked me in apprehension.

"A lot, because there is no such statement in the entire Gospel where Jesus is found teaching anything about the Trinity before he was arrested on a false charge of sedition. You can, of course, correct me if I'm wrong."

Mrs. Robinson didn't try to correct me.

So, I asked her again politely, "In that case how could we expect Jesus to command his disciples to teach something among the nations which he never taught them before?"

Mrs. Robinson preferred to remain silent.

So, I continued, "We also have no reason to guess that Jesus taught them about the Trinity in secret, or when no one was around them. I think so, because while talking to the high priest about certain charges against him, Jesus made it clear to him that he didn't teach them anything in secret or in private. Rather, he always spoke to them openly."

: Meanwhile, the high priest questioned Jesus about his disciples, and his teaching.

I have spoken openly to the world," Jesus replied. "I always taught in synagogue or at the temple, where all the Jews come together. I said nothing in secret. Why question me? Ask those who heard me. Surely they know what I said. (John 18:19–21)

"We also have no reason to guess," I continued, "That Jesus taught about the Trinity before his arrest, but the writers of the four Gospels somehow forgot to mention it. Right?

"Then why did Jesus ask his disciples to baptize all nations in the name of the Father, the Son, and the Holy Spirit, if he did not mean to worship them as one God?" Mrs. Robinson repeated her question trying to hide her frustration.

"If you don't mind listening, I can try to explain it as I understood myself after reading that verse."

"Sure. I'll be happy to know."

"Thanks. In that case, I need to tell you first what I know myself about baptism. I hope you'll correct me if you find me wrong."

"Sure."

"As far as I understand, baptism is a kind of celebration which the Christians generally observe on giving their children's name or admitting them officially in the Church, right?"

"Right."

"I also have heard that the Baptist or the Father of the Churches conducts this ceremony by dipping the child in water or by sprinkling water upon him. Is it true?"

"Yes, a child needs to go through this kind of stuff." Mrs.

Robinson admitted frankly.

"I also learned that baptism is not a mere ceremony. It has some inner or deeper meaning than admitting the child in the Church or giving his name. I learned the main purpose of baptism is to bring some changes in the heart of the children with the light or the spirit of their faith so that they could love and obey God unconditionally as did Jesus. For this reason, it is believed that baptism works better upon the older children when they understand the true meaning of the ceremony. Do you agree?"

"Yes. You are right." Mrs. Robinson affirmed.

"Thanks. Now we can try to find out what Jesus really meant when he asked his disciples to teach and baptize all nations in the name of the Father, the Son, and the Holy Spirit? As I told you before that Jesus never taught the Trinity, in that case we don't expect him to tell his disciples to teach it. I mean how could he ask them to teach something which he never taught them before?"

Mrs. Robinson remained silent.

In her silence I continued, "Now, let me explain to you what I understood myself about this command of Jesus after I read and reflected upon it. He wanted his disciples to teach the people about the true status of God whom he used to call his Father in Heaven.

"Jesus also wanted his disciples to clarify his own place and position among the people so that they could know and remember him only as a designated Prophet of God without being confused about his birth without a father, or for calling him sometimes as the Son of God.

"Similarly, Jesus also wanted his disciples to remind the people about the status of the Holy Spirit or the Chief Angel Gabriel whom God chose as one of His Messengers to carry out His commands." I stopped here for a while and took some water from my water-bottle and then asked her, "I think, I'm not boring you with my non-stop talking, right?"

"No, not at all. I'm only waiting to know why Jesus wanted his disciples to teach the people about the status of God, Jesus, and the Holy Spirit which they already knew."

"Good question. But don't lose your patience if I take some time to answer your question."

"No, I won't. Take your time."

"Thanks. I need some time because I've to explain it from both religious and geo-political situations at Jesus' time and after he left. Though Jesus knew that his people were fully aware about the highest status of God, and he or the Holy Spirit were but His obedient slaves, he wanted his disciples to keep reminding them of it. The reason is, being an inspired Messenger of God, Jesus knew about the arrival of some false prophets after him to deviate his followers from what he taught them by the command of God.

"By the false prophets Jesus meant the self-seeking religious gurus or guides who would pretend to be his true followers but joined secretly with the non-Christian Roman authority at that time to fulfill their own purpose. They knew the authority needed support from most of the people to expand their kingdom and to strenghten their rule over the land where a large number of ordinary but devoted Christians believed in One God, worshiped none but Him and tried to live their life through keeping His commands which Jesus taught them.

"They also knew the Christians were strong and united together by their faith in God and by their obedience or allegiance to Jesus. Besides that, they also had some resentment against the non-believing ruling authority. So to gain their support for the ruling authority, the so-called religious gurus needed to break their unity and to make them weak so that they could use them to serve their own purpose. Jesus also knew that they would make it happen by their invented laws which would confuse and deviate his followers from the eternal truth of the First Commandment that he preached and practiced himself when he was with them.

"At this point, it is also interesting to note that though Jesus knew about it and asked his disciples to take care of it, he also knew it was inevitable. Despite that knowledge, Jesus left for his people some precautionary notes to protect them from the blasphemous teaching of the false prophets when they arrive. I hope you know about that. Right?"

"Yes." Mrs. Robinson said in brief.

> : Beware of the false prophets, which come to you in sheep's clothing, but inwardly they are ravening wolves. (Matt. 7:15)
>
> : Take heed that no man deceives you. For many shall come in my name, saying, I am Christ; and shall deceive many. (Matt. 24:4–5)
>
> : But in vain they do worship me, teaching for doctrines the commandments of men. (Matt. 15:9)
>
> : Not everyone who says to me, Lord, Lord, will enter the kingdom of heaven, but only the one who does the will of my Father who is in heaven. (Matt. 7:21)

"In that case, we may now assume rightly what Jesus really meant when he asked his disciples to teach and baptize all nations in the name of the Father, the Son, and the Holy Spirit. He certainly didn't mean to worship the 'three' as One God. But Jesus' ascent to heaven was imminent and he had no time to give his disciples long advice or instruction. He chose two brief instructions to cover everything that he preached and practiced himself all through his life when he was with them.

"By the first instruction, Jesus wanted his disciples to teach the people not to associate anyone in the worship of God because no one is worthy of worship besides Him. And by the second instruction, he wanted them to teach the people to obey and observe everything that he taught them following the command of God in the Torah and in the Gospel."

I stopped here for a while, and then said to her, "Mrs. Robinson, I've no more to say. I've explained to you frankly what I understood myself after I read the last two verses from the last chapter in the Gospel of Matthew and from the meaning and interpretation of the Quran. If you think you have another explanation, I'd like to hear that from you."

"Maybe next time." Mrs. Robinson said while putting her Bible in the bag, and then looking at her wristwatch she asked me very politely, "Will you mind if I leave now. I have to take my father to his dentist."

"Sure. Family should come first."

The statement in 1 John 5:7 has been discarded as unauthentic

When Mrs. Robinson read the verse in 1John 5:7 in support of the Trinity, I did not know then that it was already discarded from the Revised Standard Version of the Bible as an unauthorized addition to the Greek text of the New Testament. When I first came to know about it, I tried to verify the truth in the Zondervan New International Version Bible, where it has been mentioned in a footnote that the verses 7-8 in the chapter of 1John, was not found in any Greek manuscript before the fourteenth century. The Holman Christian Standard Bible has also found it as an unauthorized addition to the Greek text of the New Testament.

In this context, I also like to remind my readers that Saint Paul-the founder of Modern Christianity and the writer of the last seventeen books of the New Testament, did not also mention anything about the Trinity in any of his books. In that case, the most obvious question is how the Trinity became an integral part of the Christian faith, if it was not taught by Jesus or by any of his disciples or even by Saint Paul who claimed to learn everything from Jesus through his vision?

The Trinity was a manmade product approved by the Council of Nicaea

While looking for the answer, I came across some authentic and well-researched books where I found the doctrine of the Trinity was a man-made product and it was approved by the council of Nicaea. I also learned that the doctrine of the Trinity was first presented by Athanasius-an Egyptian deacon from Alexandria and was accepted by the Council of Nicaea in 325 CE. It was called the Creed of Nicaea and it became an indispensable part of Christian faith about 325 years after Jesus' ascent to heaven. I have quoted below some of it from the report accepted or approved by the Council.

Whoever wishes to be saved must, above all, keep the Catholic faith.

"This is what the Catholic faith teaches: We worship one God in the Trinity and the Trinity in unity. We distinguish among the persons, but we do not divide the substance. For the Father is a distinct person; the Son is a distinct person; and the Holy Spirit is a distinct person. Still the Father and the Son and the Holy Spirit have One divinity, equal glory, and coeternal majesty. What the Father is, the Son is, and the Holy Spirit is. … The Father is eternal, the Son is eternal, and the Holy Spirit is eternal. Nevertheless, they are not three eternal beings, but one eternal being. … Likewise, the Father is omnipotent, the Son is omnipotent, and the Holy Spirit is omnipotent. Yet they are not three omnipotent beings, but one omnipotent being. Thus, the Father is God, the Son is God, and the Holy Spirit is God. But they are not three gods but one God. … For according to the Christian truth, we must profess that each of the persons individually is God; and according to Christian religion we are forbidden to say that there are three gods or lords. But the entire three persons are co-eternal and co-equal with one another."

Christian Truth is different from Christian Religion

At this point, it is interesting to note that according to the manifesto of the Council of Nicaea, the Christian truth is different from the Christian religion. The Christian truth wants its adherents to profess each of the three persons-the Father, the Son, and the Holy Spirit as a separate and independent God. But the Christian religion forbids its adherents to call them three Gods and to regard the 'three' being one, co-eternal and coequal to one another. This is how the eternal truth in the Everlasting or the First Commandment of God (Gen. 17:7, Duet. 6:4-5, Mark. 12:29-30), which was pure and pristine monotheism, got contaminated with the pagan practice of polytheism and became assimilated with the Christian faith in the name of Jesus.

The doctrine of the Trinity was rejected by the Unitarian Christians

But we have no reason to believe that Jesus' true followers-the Unitarian Christians or the worshipers of One True God, accepted the doctrine of the Trinity as they were commanded to do by the polytheist Roman Authority at that time. According to the authentic report of the historians and the open-minded religious scholars, we came to know they rejected it at once to be wrong, inappropriate, and above all, as a grave sin of blasphemy against the oneness of God.

When the Authority or the Council failed to justify their doctrine through logic, evidence, or acceptable explanation, they tried to force them to accept it blindly. Not only that they also began to arrest, torture, burn, and to crucify them inhumanly who dared to oppose the council or to criticize their doctrine in public. Many of them were also reported to leave their home and hearth and began to live in the desolate forest or in the caves of mountains only to save their faith from the tyranny of their oppressors.

But, it is also a fact that by the end of the fourth century, the doctrine of the Trinity became assimilated as an indispensable part of the Christian faith, and since then, the devoted followers of Jesus Christ have been worshiping God in the union of three by ignoring the crystal-clear message of the First Commandment that Jesus taught them himself and which they still find in the Gospel-the Book they love to claim as a true account of Jesus' own words and deeds.

The Quran has denounced the Trinity as a clear blaspheme against the oneness of God

My Christian friends may feel surprised to know that the Quran which God sent to His last and final Prophet Muhammad about six hundred years after Jesus' ascent to heaven, also testifies that Jesus never taught the Trinity. Not only that, the Quran has also denounced the doctrine of the Trinity as a grave sin of blasphemy against the oneness of God. I have quoted below a few of those verses to justify my claim.

: O people of the Book! [Meaning the Christians who received the Gospel through Jesus] Do not transgress on the limits of your religion. Speak nothing but the truth about Allah. The Messiah Jesus-the son of Mary was no more than a Messenger of Allah and His word 'Be' which He bestowed upon Mary and a Spirit from Him. So, believe in Allah and His Messenger and do not say Trinity. Stop saying that. Allah is only One Deity. (4:171)

: Certainly, they have disbelieved who say: "Allah is Christ-the son of Mary while Christ himself said, "O children of Israel! Worship Allah; my Lord and your Lord.' whoever commits shirk [to worship God in association with others], Allah will deny him paradise, and the hellfire will be his home. They disbelieve who say: "God is one of the 'three' in a Trinity." For, there is no god except One God. If they desist not from what they say, verily a grievous chastisement will befall the disbelievers among them. (5:72-73)

: Remember! when Allah said: "O Jesus! I will take you and raise you to Myself and clear you of those who disbelieve. I will make those superior who follow you to those who disbelieve until the Day of Resurrection. Then you all will return to Me and I will judge between you in the matters wherein you differ. (3:55)

My own reflection on the Trinity which most of the Christian believe today as a way to their salvation

Sometimes I think, if the members of the Council of Nicaea had any idea that God would send His last prophet Muhammad glorifying and testifying of Jesus's true status, and clearing his name from all the lies and falsehood in His everlasting Guidebook-the Quran, they might have thought twice before they dared inventing anything in his name or to demean his role and mission as a unique and a special Messenger of God.

Sometimes, I feel truly surprised when I think how could the Christians of the Modern World both the elite and the ordinary follow this kind of ambiguous, illogical, and invented doctrine of men as a key to their salvation against the clear, consistent, and the straight path of God which they still find in the teaching of Jesus and all his predecessors who were sent before him?

Sometimes, I feel the urge to ask them who is now forcing or persecuting them to worship One God in the union of Three or Three Gods as One when they know very well that Jesus never taught the Trinity, rather he always commanded them to worship none but One God as did all his Predecessors before him?

Sometimes, I want to ask them straight what makes them reject Muhammad when they know he is the only Prophet of God who arrived after Jesus with the Quran confirming his role, mission and teaching which they still find in the Gospel-the Book they believe themselves as a true account of Jesus' own words and deeds?

But I never asked them any of those questions, because I know religion is a very sensitive subject. While listening to the sermons of some well-reputed evangelists and their prayer to God in the name of the Father, the Son and the Holy Spirit for their salvation, I still pray to my Almighty Lord to open their hearts and to help them to realize the truth that He revealed through all His prophets beginning from Adam to His last Prophet Muhammad.

: It is not possible for a man whom Allah has given the Book, the Wisdom and the Prophethood that he would say to the people: Worship me instead of Allah. On the contrary he would say to the people: "Be worshipers of your Lord in accordance with the Holy Book you have been teaching and reading. Nor would he command you to take the angels and the prophets as your Lords. (Quran 3:79–80)

BIBLIOGRAPHY

1. King James Versions: Thomas Nelson Publisher
2. New Revised Standard Versions: The Harper Collins Study Bible, Harper San Francisco
3. New International Version: Zondervan, Michigan
4. English Translation from the Quranic Text: By Ali, A, Yusuf; Pickthal & Shafi Muhammad Mufti
5. The Concise Encyclopedia of Islam. By Glasse Cyril, Harper Collins, New York
6. Merriam-Webster's Encyclopedia of World Religions, Springfield, MA, 1999
7. The Christianity of Jesus: By Backwell, R. H, 1972
8. Christianity on Trial: By Chapman, Colin, 1974
9. The God of early Christians: By MacGiffert, 1924
10. A History of the Early Church: By Leitzman, Hanz, 1961
11. Council of Nicaea and St. Athanasius: By Corelli, Marie, 1898
12. What did Jesus really say? By Abdullah Mishaal Ibn, 1996
13. The Bible's Last Prophet. By Siddiqui Faisal, 1995
14. Muhammad in the Bible. By Badawi Jamal, 2005
15. What does the Bible say about Muhammad? By Ahmed Deedat, 1998
16. Izhar-Ul-Haq (Truth Revealed) Part 1-4, By M.M. Rahamatullah, 1992 37
17. The Dead Sea Scroll, The Gospel of Barnabas, and The New Testament, By M.A.Yussef, 1994

ABOUT THE AUTHOR

The author, Dil R Banu is a Muslim by birth and practice and a retired lecturer from a prestigious school and college in her homeland Bangladesh. She settled in America as an immigrant more than three decades ago. She worked as a substitute teacher for a year or so, and then began to operate a licensed family day-care in her rented apartment where all her neighbours were Christians. This job was a turning point in her life because it made her a writer from a day-care provider.

During this period, she met with many Christian missionaries with whom she had transformative interactions. Their discussions were fascinating exchanges that centered around God, the Bible, and the Quran. Owing to her openness, and a warm personality, she has forged lasting bonds with many Christians and continues enlightening exchanges with them.

She thinks our faith in God, which we usually inherit through our parents and remain stuck to it from our early age as the only to our salvation, is like riding a bus without knowing whether it will take us to our destination but believing it will. Though the riders on a wrong bus have a chance to correct their mistakes, but the believers in God who follow their faith believing to reach their desired goal, are not that lucky. They have no chance at all to correct their mistakes once they cross the one-way exit of death and find them in a wrong place. So she thinks as our worldly life is short and uncertain, it is better and safer for all of us, the sooner we identify the true path of God and try to pursue it until the last moment of our life.

Though she did her Masters in Bengali literature, her favorite subjects are Comparative religion, Philosophy and History. She also enjoys travelling, praying, and passing time with her family, friends and grandchildren.

ABOUT THE BOOK

The title of the book makes it clear about the contents of the book. She wrote this book from her previously published book "ONE GOD FOR ALL" putting special emphasis on what Jesus taught his people himself himself about their way to heaven by the command of God and what he never taught.

It is written mainly for the devoted Christians who worship One God in the union of three, popularly known as Trinity. This book might surprise them if they know that Jesus never taught them the Trinity. Not only that, the Gospel which they claim as a true account of Jesus' own words and deeds, does not contain a single statement where he asked his people to worship him as God or as one of the Gods in the Trinity. Naturally, because the Trinity was a man-made doctrine and it became an indispensable part of their faith and a way to their salvation nearly four hundred years after Jesus' ascent to Heaven.

The inquisitive and the truth-seeking readers may find this book interesting, informative and worth reading.

Pacific book review on author's first book

ONE GOD FOR ALL

By Rae C. Bernard

There is always a comparison and contrast to both spiritual texts, between the Bible and the Quran, on whose God is better or most powerful. Surprisingly, the debate will forever remain between JudeoChristians and Muslims, until both sides become more open-minded to the possibility of a One God, no matter what name is preferred for reference. In One God for All, author Dil R. Banu ensures readers that God is one and the same regardless of what another religion, specifically of Islam, is calling Him, by providing evidence from both spiritual texts. People are always trying to prove there is a difference between what they believe versus others they encounter and this book demonstrates otherwise. By reading this book, you will gain a level of open mindfulness. Maybe there is more than what you've been raised or taught to believe. You learn that the text in both the Quran and the Bible share unexpected similarities, especially for someone who has never read both books of spiritual texts.

Jesus and Muhammad are the most important individuals in each book because they are the last of God/Allah's messengers for the people on earth. One would be fascinated in learning that both messengers were created to fulfill similar purposes. This grants the ability to step outside of your in-box thinking and consider the proof provided to you, encouraging the overall goal of a One God for everyone. Of course, one would think because there are different books, there would be different views on what is believed and it's not the case with this book. Not once has the author critiqued or opted to project her views onto the readers, setting the reading experience in more of an educational tone.

The author used letters as a method to educate readers, which shows various correspondences with a reverence about specific Holy Scriptures. This enables clarity for those assuming that the beliefs of Muslims are not the same as those of Judeo-Christians. It is a true eye-opener discovering that prophets and messengers had a particular task to aid the evolving world and its inhabitants. Either beliefs want its people to remain on a righteous path, following the rules/commandments of God/Allah or it is up to the individuals to uphold their end of the agreement.

I have never had the opportunity to read the Quran in my entire life; I was amazed by the way their text had instances like the Bible. In learning this, I started to come to understand just how strong the Islamic beliefs are and why they seem hardcore to do anything in the name of Allah. I felt that I can take away quite a few scriptures from the Quran that are in agreement with the Bible and know that they too want the same thing for their lives and their people. I am very appreciative of the author for delving into both books and finding scriptures from each to aid her case that we all believe in One God, and only one alone.

The book is well-written with personal research, spending time in gathering the proper evidence to provide clarity to readers. I highly recommend anyone who wants to discover for themselves just how similar both spiritual books can be to consider reading One God for All, as the author saved her readers time and the necessity for having to read both.

ANNA ASKED WAS MUHAMMAD A PROPHET?

[Her question is answered from the Bible and
other major scriptures of the world]

By Aaron Washington

Author Dil R. Banu first started by defining what prophecy is. I was impressed with her detailed explanation as it made me have a deeper understanding of the definition and why God's people are referred to as prophets. There are so many people who claim to be prophets in today's world. This can be confusing to believers who follow anyone who proclaims the word. The author further expounded on the subject of false prophecy with a Bible verse (Deut 18:21-22). Through that verse, we learn the true prophets make correct prophesies, but it is God who inspires them. False prophets, on the other hand, rely on their imagination, making them fail most of the time.

Dil R. Banu's intent when writing Anna Asked Was Muhammad a Prophet was to show the link between Muhammad and the prophets in the Bible. Christianity and Islam may operate on a different basis, but the fact remains that there are some fundamental beliefs in both the Quran and the Bible which link the two. This is what the author wants everyone to understand. Anna Asked Was Muhammad a Prophet, is a religious book which helps even the unobservant and least interested readers know more about religion and Prophet Muhammad. It is amazing how the author broke everything down. I learned much about Islam teachings vis-a-vis the Christian gospel by the end of my read.

One of the most fascinating parts in the book was when the author explained the relation between Muhammad, Jesus, and Moses. Contrary to popular belief, Muhammad was not like Jesus. He was more like Moses. This is because Jesus was born of the Virgin Mary, in a miraculous way. Both Moses and Muhammad, however, were born to a married couple. The two later got married and had their own offspring. The next comparison between Moses and Muhammad versus Jesus was that the two were accepted, obeyed, and respected by most of their people as the true messengers of God in their own lifetime. This was not the case with Jesus. Jews rejected Jesus and his mission and even claimed that he was not the true Messiah.

Dil R. Banu's discussion of the three brought about a lot of clarity to this history. At the end of the day, I was able to tell the three apart and noted the roles they played. Reading Anna Asked Was Muhammad a Prophet, gave me the impression of going through the Bible and the Quran simultaneously.

The author did a fantastic job by writing this book as it helped me have a better understanding of the two books. Dil R. Banu's book is nothing short of informative. The author is engaging too and wrote from an informed point of view. Other than her way of explaining things, I have to mention the author's choice of words was another thing that made this book easy to read. The language used is simple with the exception of a few technical words which are well outlined in the text. This book is ideal for a wide range of reading audiences from early adult on up, and of virtually any faith, with any degree of religious background.

ABRAHAM WAS COMMANDED TO SACRIFICE ISHMAEL-HIS FIRSTBORN

By Md Mahbubur Rahman, Ph.D.

"Anna Asked, Was Muhammad a Prophet?" is an appealing exploration of religious history and theological inquiry that investigates deeply into the lives and legacies of key biblical and Quranic figures. The book addresses a profound question posed by the author's friend, Anna, about the prophet Muhammad, and it thoughtfully examines the intersections of Judaism, Christianity, and Islam.

The author begins by recounting her close friendship with Anna, which provides a heartfelt and personal backdrop to the book. Their age and ethnic differences only deepen their bond, highlighting the universal nature of their inquiry. The question that sparked the book— about Muhammad's prophetic status—leads the author into a broader exploration of another contentious issue: which of Abraham's sons was intended for sacrifice.

Through meticulous study and comparison of the Bible, the Quran, and Jewish, Christian, and Islamic traditions, the author unravels the narrative of Abraham's commanded sacrifice. This pivotal episode, shared yet differently interpreted across these faiths, forms the core of the book. The author's investigation into whether Isaac or Ishmael was the intended son is both scholarly and accessible, offering readers a thorough understanding of the historical and theological context.

The book stands out for its balanced and respectful approach. The author emphasizes that her goal is not to undermine anyone's faith but to seek clarity and truth. Her narrative is enriched by personal stories, especially her reaction to online posts that mischaracterize Abraham, Hagar, and Ishmael, and her heartfelt shock at the hostility she found.

One of the book's strengths is its ability to engage readers of all backgrounds. The author's detailed examination of Abraham's story encourages readers to consider the deep-rooted connections and differences among the Abrahamic faiths. Her writing is not just informative but also thought-provoking, inviting readers to reflect on their beliefs and the historical narratives they hold dear.

The discussion about the defamation against Abraham and his family, the misinterpretation of Ishmael's status, and the subsequent rejection of Muhammad as a prophet provides a fresh perspective on age-old controversies. The author's use of scripture and tradition to support her arguments is compelling and well-researched, making the book a valuable resource for anyone interested in interfaith dialogue.

In conclusion, "Anna Asked, Was Muhammad a Prophet?" is an enlightening and profound read. It challenges readers to look beyond their predetermined notions and encourages a deeper understanding of shared religious heritage. The author's sincere and humble approach makes this book not just a scholarly endeavor but a heartfelt journey toward truth and understanding. It is a must-read for anyone interested in the rich tapestry of Abrahamic traditions and the quest for interfaith harmony.

Author's other books

1. ONE GOD FOR ALL
2. ANNA ASKED WAS MUHAMMAD A PROPHET?
   [Her question is answered from the Bible, the Quran and other major scriptures of the world]
3. JESUS' COMFORTER IS MUHAMMAD, THE LAST PROPHET OF GOD
4. ABRAHAM WAS COMMANDED TO SACRIFICE ISHMAEL, HIS FIRSTBORN

Author's next books

1. OUR ONLY WAY TO HEAVEN AS DESCRIBED IN BOTH BIBLE AND QURAN
2. ISLAM - THE TERMINATOR OF ALL EVILS

Written in reply to Evangelist Franklin Graham's comment on Islam being a very evil and a very wicked religion.]

Visit Author's Website on www.godinbibleandquran.com

9 798889 175196 5